Natural Flower Arranging

Natural
Flower Arranging

Mary Adams

B T Batsford Limited, London

To Diccon and in memory of Rick who prepared many of my wedding flowers for me to arrange

First published 1981
ISBN 0 7134 2677 2

Filmset by Willmer Brothers Limited
Birkenhead, Merseyside

Printed in Great Britain by
The Anchor Press Ltd.
Tiptree, Essex
For the publishers
B T Batsford Limited
4 Fitzhardinge Street
London W1H 0AH

Contents

Acknowledgment

My special thanks go to Diccon for his constant help and advice, superb line drawings and photography. Also a very special thank you to Thelma M. Nye of Batsford for her great interest and excellent advice which made this book possible.

Without the very lovely line drawings of my work from Mary Agnes Lansdowne in California the book would not be the same and I would like to thank her, Barbara Bearden and Jean Dew very much indeed for their great enthusiasm and help over the prospect of the book.

I would also like to thank Lady Pulbrook, Sonia Waites, all my friends and students and last, but not least, the Staff of Pulbrook and Gould, Sloane Street, London for their interest in the project.

The line drawings are by Mary Agnes Lansdowne, Art Associates of California; Diccon Adams, Dipl. Arch; and Felicity Black.

The photographs were taken by Diccon Adams; Carolyn Caddes, Palo Alto, California; Commercial Studios, Ipswich; David Eaton, Pacific Grove, California; Roy Fraser; Jim Geiger, Mercury News, California; and Pipe and Rich Ltd.

London 1981   M. A.

Preface

Mary Adams's book will have a special appeal to all those who have a love of the country and of the wild flowers and grasses which grow in our fields and hedgerows.

There is today, I think, a feeling for the need to return to simplicity in design – the elaborate and formal flower arrangements of the past look out of place in our smaller and more simply furnished houses.

As a country-lover Mary Adams brings to all her flower arrangements a feeling of freshness and simplicity. The use of 'old fashioned' garden flowers – often a mixture of wild flowers and grasses – gives the effect of a cottage garden brought into a house.

Mary Adams and I have worked together and always shared this love of simple wild flowers and so I wish her all good fortune.

London 1981

Susan Pulbrook

Introduction

The flowers in silence seem to breathe
Such thoughts as language cannot tell.

From *The Language of Flowers* compiled and edited by Mrs L. Burke

Many of my students have asked me to write a book which is not technical; a book which they could pick up when they were tired, read a little, look at a lot and feel refreshed. This is the result; I hope you will enjoy it.

Life for me began in Ceylon, now Sri Lanka, where my father was a tea planter. I asked my Sinhalese nanny where I had come from; she told me my mother had found me in the garden in a bed of cannas! From then on flowers and colour seemed very important to my life.

Our garden was very beautiful; my mother had many talents and one was landscape gardening. She planted a magnificent variety of flowers and shrubs, orchids, bougainvillea, moon flowers, oleanders, lantana and many many more. She brought the garden indoors with glorious arrangements in bowls with chicken wire to hold them in position. She arranged plants and ferns in groups on the verandahs of the bungalow – it was all quite magical and a lovely background in which to be growing up. I used to help her in the garden and also translated her instructions into Sinhalese to pass on to the gardeners – a language which I spoke fluently, thanks to my nanny. The importance of flowers and plants followed me through schooling in England and into adulthood. I realised you could bring happiness with a bunch of flowers and change a whole sad day for someone into a happier day. My housemistress at boarding school used to make us go for cycle rides on a Saturday to woods to collect flowers, then on Sunday after church, we would go to the hospital to give them to patients. They were thrilled with the gift; the smiles and the cheery good mornings showed the importance of the psychology of flowers.

I trained to be a teacher and it was not until after I married that I did anything serious about my hobby, flower arranging. I decided to do a floristry course so that I could make bouquets for my friends' weddings in Ceylon. This training did, in fact, stand me in good stead when we left Ceylon to begin a new life in England with a flower business in Suffolk. This was followed by teaching flower arranging and floristry all the year round in London for sixteen years.

I hope to show with this book of flower arranging that a natural style is fun and certainly as artistic as anything too stylized and measured. It brings out the individual's own ideas of colour combinations and planning. When I teach I try to encourage originality and it is wonderful to see this actually taking place as each person works at her arrangement.

Planning

When I arrange I try to choose a balanced mixture of flowers and foliage. Some should be light and dainty such as jasmin, honeysuckle, petrea, congea, broom; some heavier and more sculptured such as lilies, roses, clematis and spathiphyllum. If I am arranging a bowl of all one kind of flower I pick or choose buds or small blooms for the outside area of the arrangement and half open and fully open blooms for the centre of the design.

Always buy extra flowers to keep aside for repairs at a later date. It is important to have a light and airy look for the end result – so light that a butterfly could fly through in England or a hummingbird in California. They fly around us as we work and enjoy the nectar from our flowers.

It is important to get a three dimensional look to the arrangement so that the eye travels to the heart of the design. It is similar to sculpture; try to get the depth needed to make the design more exciting. It is simple to arrange a fan with no heart but so exciting to get some space into one's effort. This effect can be achieved with two or three special leaves, *Hosta, Diffenbachia, Begonia rex*, or some short flowers recessed deep into the arrangement.

Flowers can look dramatic if they are arranged in a niche on top of glass and lit from below with a tiny low watt bulb. Equally attractive is a spotlight shining down onto the arrangement as one does with beautiful paintings, but with the heat of the light the flowers will soon fade.

Never leave buying, cutting and arranging your flowers until the last possible moment. This is a terrible mistake. Get all the chicken wire filling of containers done the week before they are going to be needed; it is amazing how long this takes. Make sure your vases are spotlessly clean; I am constantly amazed at the way people will put a dirty container away in the cupboard. When you throw away the old flowers, clean the vase before putting it away. Bacteria forms in the vase if it is left dirty, which will attack your fresh flowers so that they will not last. I usually wash my containers with a special stiff brush and a little disinfectant in the soapy water. The chicken wire should also be kept clean in each container as bacteria will collect there and kill your flowers.

Planning

So think well ahead of time about the various flower arrangements, visit your flower shop and see what there is available. Take a list of your requirements with you and ask if it will be possible to get everything you need when you want them; substitute with other varieties if anything is unobtainable.

Arrange your flowers two or three days before a party so that you can enjoy the experience and not be harrassed by all the last minute details. Remember to fill the container twice daily: just a topping up is all that is necessary and a light spray from a fine mister. Care must be taken of precious furniture and wallpaper, so make sure that these items are protected before you spray.

When arranging try if possible to work in the room where the flowers are eventually going to be. Take a neat dust sheet to put down and keep as tidy as possible. Half fill your vase then arrange in position and finally top up with more water and spray gently. By doing this you are aware, as you arrange, of the lights, pictures and other objects in the room – all of which have to be considered in the final plan. Also, a most important point, you are arranging at the correct height of the finished arrangement.

For parties it is advisable to have a few large arrangements placed high and out of the way of bruising by excited people. An entrance hall arrangement to greet people, one or two large ones in the reception room and a dressing table arrangement in the bedroom are all important.

Normally I use 2 in./5 cm chicken wire for any flower work but for arrangements for weddings and parties it is a good idea to use well soaked *Oasis* covered with a cage of chicken wire and tied down with reel wire, 28 gauge/0·38 mm. If the flower arrangements have to be transported or carried from one room to another they are probably more stable in the *Oasis* than in chicken wire alone. A good flower arrangement, however, will not have any movement of flowers even in chicken wire alone but this does need years of practice and experience.

In your planning time, remember the flowers and foliage are going to need all night to drink in deep water if picked in the evening, or all day if picked in the early morning. I usually spray the flowers and foliage whilst they are having their conditioning drink and very often place sprayed tissue paper over

them to keep a constant moist cool atmosphere.

Always take a bucket of water into the garden and place your cut stems straight into this; it helps the long lasting of flowers enormously. I am sure it is best in really hot weather to cut very early in the morning as the night dew and cool air is beneficial to all flowers and foliage. They can be conditioned all day and arranged in the cool of the evening – you will be amazed at how long they will last if treated carefully in this way.

Spring flowers

This is a photograph of a corner of my Suffolk flower shop showing the bamboo screen against the wall which could frequently be changed to various other colour schemes.

I used a great many antique containers for the shop arrangements as well as modern handmade ones. Victorian scales, glass dome and lantern can all be seen here, also an antique Chinese jar filled with lilac and *Grevillea* or silver oak.

Spring flowers

A few sprays of special blossom can be arranged on a pinholder to give a really natural look. Let one or two branches curve over the rim of the container allowing a bloom or an attractive group of leaves to hide the pinholder and give weight to the arrangement. For the three branches of *Magnolia soulangeana* I used a white dish and two pinky glass spheres which floated in the water. It is important to keep the water spotlessly clean and dust free.

Spring flowers

A friend gave me some beautiful branches of *Magnolia soulangeana* from her nursery garden. I slit the stem ends and put them in deep water overnight and then arranged them in my Lady with her wheelbarrow. The pink hyacinths were cut from the garden to tuck in below the magnolia flowers. This made a 'welcome home' arrangement standing on a carved camphorwood chest in the entrance hall of my home.

A small country church is a joy in which to arrange flowers and this was for a spring wedding in Suffolk.

I arranged, at each side of the altar, two matching Isles of Scilly handmade urns, but at slightly different levels.

The foliage frame was of the beautiful *Ruscus* and ivy trails. Added to this were sprays of forsythia. Arum lilies of various sizes flowed through the arrangement, also yellow carnations, white tulips 'Pax', and yellow and white narcissi 'Ice Follies'.

Spring flowers

At the entrance of a small Suffolk church, near Hadleigh, I arranged this hamper basket for a wedding. Well crumpled 2 in./5 cm chicken wire was placed in the zinc lining and it was then filled with water. The foliage frame was *Ruscus* and five sprays of the beautiful *Magnolia soulangeana* 'Alba'. Into this frame fourteen arum lilies flowed through the arrangement and twenty *Narcissi actea* which have a delightful perfume.

Wedding Design

This photograph shows a student's table set out for a day of floristry in Wedding Design. There are the stub wires, reel wire and scissors. The carnations and orchids are in water ready for making up. To the left can be seen the blooms of roses, freesias, sprays of orchids wired and covered in gutta percha ready to be made up into a curved shower bouquet.

My students share a large table for this work and around the studio room there are plenty of mirrors for actually making up their bouquets. It is important to look into the mirror as you assemble the flowers as this is how the bouquet will eventually be seen.

Although the majority of brides will call upon the professional services of a florist for their wedding bouquets and bridesmaids' posies, there are many flower arrangers who may like to experiment with this type of flower arranging. For these I have included a number of simple spring and summer bouquet designs.

NOTES ON BOUQUET WORK

The most important point is to make sure the flowers chosen for making the bouquet are really long-lasting.

Never use wild flowers as they wilt extremely quickly when out of water. Try to avoid using too many strongly perfumed flowers; this can cause a bride to feel faint in the church, where the smell of flowers will be strong anyway from the arrangements around the church.

Blossom is also short lived, so my advice is avoid it for bouquets. Sweet peas are popular but the bouquet must be made on the day of the wedding, and preferably not in heat wave conditions.

Roses should be bought in tight bud and florists' varieties are the best, not garden roses as these tend to blow open very quickly indeed. Roses can be pinned very carefully with fine reel wire if the weather is very hot during summer months. See diagram overleaf.

If in doubt it is a good idea to experiment beforehand. Make up an identical bouquet, spray it and box down in a cool room – see how long it lasts and be guided by your experiments.

When discussing the flowers with the bride, make sure you have a second choice of flower in case her favourite is unobtainable. Remember that during busy wedding periods, such as Easter, Whitsun, September and Christmas, white flowers will probably be scarce.

Care must be taken when making buttonholes to make sure that the stem ends of flowers are covered with gutta percha as sap does stain. Some flowers are far worse than others for staining. The Arum lily is probably one of the worst as it is a dull rust colour and extremely difficult to remove. Sometimes one is asked for an Arum lily natural stemmed sheaf, in which case cover the stem ends with green gutta percha to match exactly the green of the lily stem.

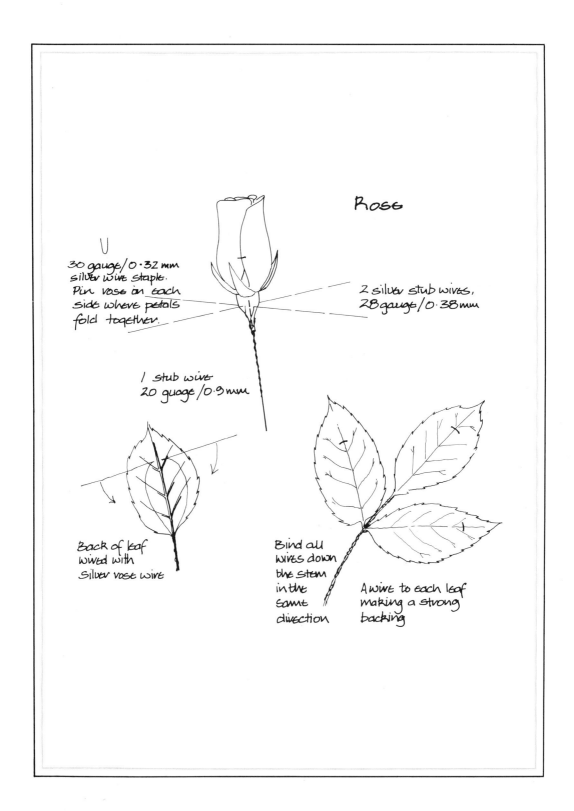

Rose

30 gauge/0·32 mm
silver wire staple.
Pin rose on each
side where petals
fold together.

2 silver stub wires,
28 gauge/0·38 mm

1 stub wire
20 gauge/0·9 mm

Back of leaf
wired with
silver rose wire

Bind all
wires down
the stem
in the
same
direction

A wire to each leaf
making a strong
backing

Springtime bouquets

A sweet smelling bouquet of pipped hyacinths is one of the loveliest of spring bouquets. The term pipped means each individual flower taken off the main stem and wired with fine stub wire 35 gauge. This one was shaded from palest pink to deep pink with a touch of soft blue near the centre area of the curving spray.

Each hyacinth flower is wired with a fine silver stub wire hooked into its trumpet and down the base of the flower. Each is then covered with gutta percha and finally mounted, in threes, onto a 14 in./35 cm long, 22 gauge/0·71 mm stub wire, which is also covered with gutta percha.

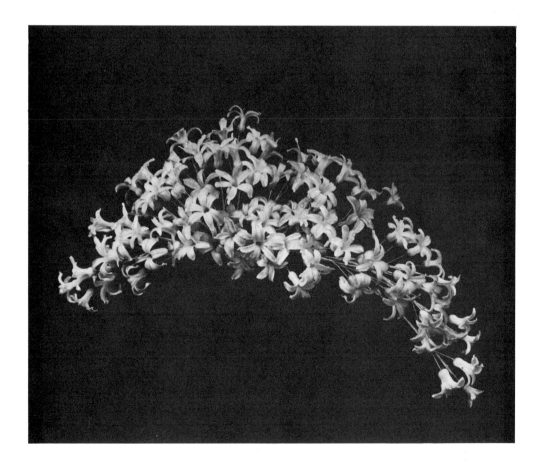

24

Springtime bouquets

The bride was a tall beautiful model wearing a very full skirted lace dress and long veil. I designed the bouquet especially for her using *Eucharis lilies* in the centre, graduating out to white freesias and lily of the valley. The foliage is the variegated *Euonymus E fortunei* 'Silver Queen' with some pale green lily of the valley leaves.

Eucharis lilies grow with their heads hanging down and the beautiful pale green centres are only seen when you hold the heads up and look into them.

When wired for bouquet making these are seen to great effect and people often ask what the flowers are as they look so entirely different from the way they do when growing. They are free flowering in Ceylon and I used them frequently for my wedding work but of course in England they are considered to be very special and are comparatively rare.

Freesias are wired first with fine silver reel wire along each stem, round each flower and bud until the top bud is reached. Give a little final twist before cutting reel wire.

The *Eucharis lily* is wired by placing a small bud of cotton wool on the top of a hooked 22 gauge/0·71 mm stub wire 14 in./35 cm long and inserting it down the throat of the flower into the stem, pull down and cover with gutta percha.

Lily of the valley is wired with fine silver reel wire up the stem and round each bell until the top bud is reached. Give a little twist then cut reel wire.

All the flowers are mounted with a 22 gauge/0·71 mm stub wire 14 in./35 cm long, and covered with white gutta percha.

Springtime bouquets

This is one of my fun bouquets which I made up in a spare moment – it was to become a 'best seller': ten lily of the valley for daintiness at each end, a touch of cream freesia, just five stems, and centre of cream tulips. The three tulips at the heart of the bouquet were opened gently and the remaining seven tulips were placed around the centre three. My favourite fern is the *Nephrolepsis* variety which I used with three variegated *Hosta* leaves in the centre, near the open tulips. The ladder fern is wired with fine silver reel wire up the stem until the top is reached, then the wire is twisted and cut. To condition the fern it should be placed under water for 30 minutes and then stood upright in deep water overnight.

Freesias are wired up the stem and round each flower with fine silver wire.

Tulips have 2 × 22 gauge/0·71 mm stub wire 14 in./35 cm long, up the stem and secured across the stem with reel wire.

All wired stems are covered with gutta percha.

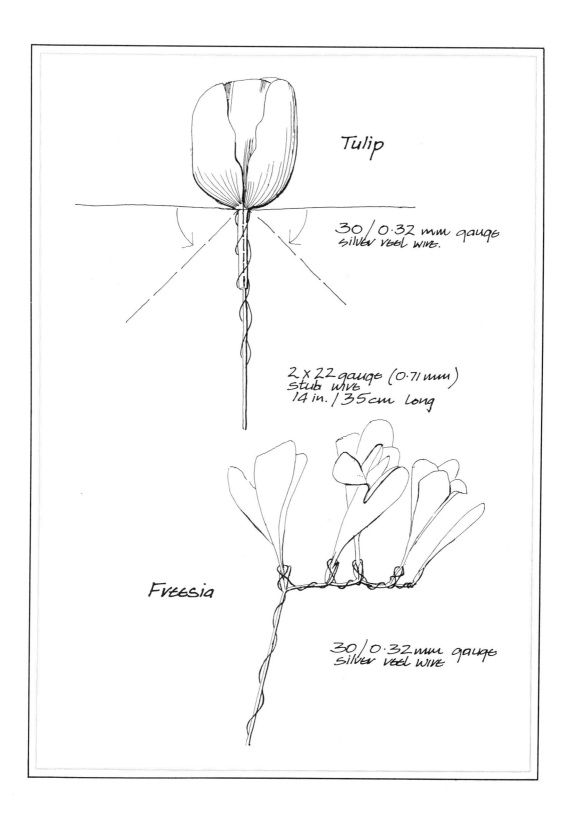

Tulip

30 / 0.32 mm gauge
silver reel wire.

2 x 22 gauge (0.71 mm)
stub wire
14 in. / 35 cm long

Freesia

30 / 0.32 mm gauge
silver reel wire

28

Springtime bouquets

Short brides and bridesmaids must have small and dainty bouquets. This one is totally springlike and the perfume is extremely delicate.

Twenty sprays of lily of the valley and fifteen stems of freesias are necessary in this bouquet. The foliage is *Peperomia hederefolia* which is a really dark green and looks beautiful against the white flowers and pale green leaves of the lily of the valley. The freesias are arranged so that the biggest blooms are in the centre of the bouquet, smaller blooms flowing out to the sides and tails. The lily of the valley looks prettiest at the end and on the outside edges, with just a touch arranged near the centre.

Finish the bouquet handle with ribbon bound neatly, finally attach a small bow at the top of the handle.

Springtime bouquets

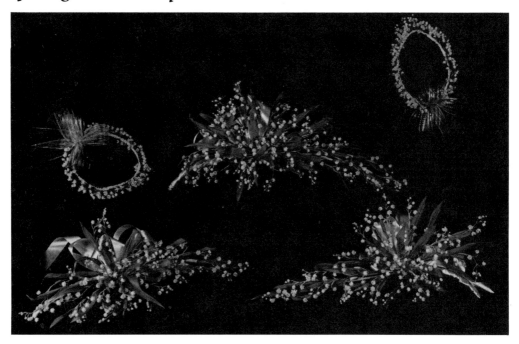

Quite the prettiest of all spring bouquets are made entirely of lily of the valley. This group of three, for one of my Suffolk brides and her two bridesmaids, were shaped in a slightly curving shower. Each bouquet had six dozen lily of the valley plus their own light green leaves. The whole arrangement has to be light and airy; slim dainty stems at the ends of the bouquet with the fuller blooms in the centre. Ribbon bows of palest green are placed at the back of the bouquet to finish the handle.

Each headdress consists of thirty stems of lily of the valley. Each stem was cut to half the full length and wired with fine reel wire to make tiny dainty sprays which were bound onto white chenille wire to make a circlet. Ribbon bows in pale green were finally attached to be seen at the back of the head.

Lily of the valley is carefully wired with finest reel wire 34 gauge/0·28 mm. Take the wire up each stem in between the bells until the top bud is reached, then give a final twist and cut reel wire.

Mount the lily of the valley stem plus leaf onto a 22 gauge/0·71 mm stub wire 14 in./35 cm long, and cover with gutta percha.

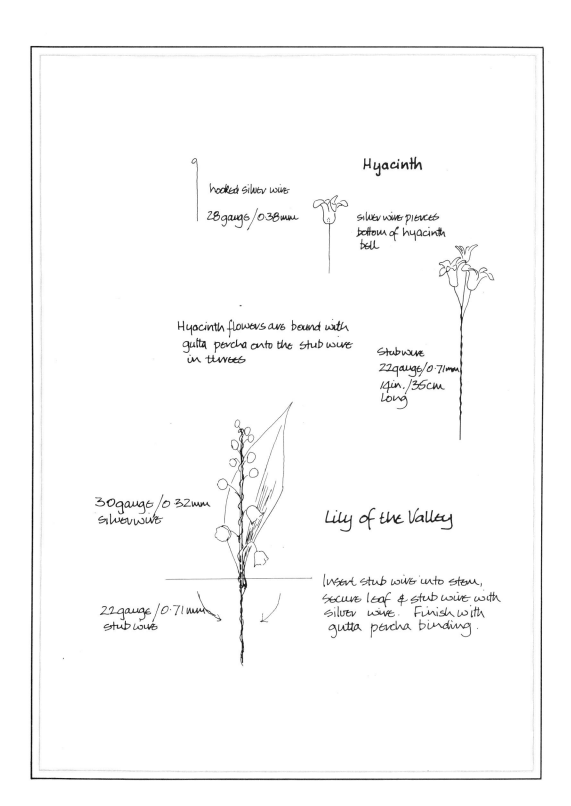

Hyacinth

hooked silver wire
28 gauge / 0·38 mm

silver wire pierces
bottom of hyacinth
bell

Hyacinth flowers are bound with
gutta percha onto the stub wire
in threes

Stub wire
22 gauge / 0·71 mm
14 in. / 35 cm
Long

30 gauge / 0·32 mm
silver wire

Lily of the Valley

22 gauge / 0·71 mm
stub wire

Insert stub wire into stem,
secure leaf & stub wire with
silver wire. Finish with
gutta percha binding.

Summer flowers

When I go into the garden to pick a bouquet I
usually arrange the flowers in my hand as I pick.
You will have decided on the container and the
room to be decorated, therefore you know
your colour scheme. The rest is easy. Pick
dainty taller flowers such as *Thalictrum
dipterocarpum* 'Hewitt's Double', *Phlox
adsurgens* and *Gerberas* – the phlox is just right
for the intermediate area and the *Gerbera* for
the centre as they are the bigger flowers.

The same applies to cutting foliage for an
arrangement, dainty ferns, ivies or honeysuckle for
the outside edges and heavier varieties such as *Arum
italicum, Hosta, Begonia rex* for the centre area. Phlox can
have an overpowering scent especially when in a confined space.

Just an attractive handful of beautiful
border carnations, which have a slight,
but very pleasant perfume.

CREATING AN ARRANGEMENT
Stages one and two

This arrangement was to be long and fairly narrow for a dinner party of fourteen guests. I used an ordinary oval plain glass pyrex dish as it was going to stand in a silver entree dish on the dinner table.

First, several layers of 2 in./5 cm chicken wire were crumpled and secured with reel wire at each side and each end. Half fill with water before beginning to arrange, then add more water when the arrangement is finished. For each end I used the long spiky *Nephrolepis exaltata* 'Sword Fern' and at the sides maidenhair fern – this was my foliage outline.

Into this 'frame' of foliage I gradually added the flowers from the garden, sprays of jasmine, some side shoots of pale blue delphinium and some long sprays of a pale pink bougainvillea.

Conditioning of bougainvillea
Take off all leaves, gently hammer stem ends and submerge in very slightly warm water.

34

Stages three and four

The filling in of the design continues with pink sweet peas flowing from one end to the other in a soft diagonal line, and pale mauve sweet peas flowing in the opposite direction, again diagonally.

Finally five blooms of pale mauve clematis 'Nelly Moser' were added, again placed diagonally (two at one side and three on the other side). To give a feeling of depth referred to as recession I tucked in a few short sprays of bougainvillea and jasmine to hide any visible areas of chicken wire.

Conditioning of clematis
Cut at dawn, hammer stem ends very gently and stand in water up to the bloom for at least three hours or better still all morning. Some people like to dip the stem ends into boiling water for a second before giving the long drink but I found my blooms lasted well with the first method. Always experiment as different varieties may respond to different methods. I have heard some people like to give clematis champagne for their first drink but as yet I have not tried this method!

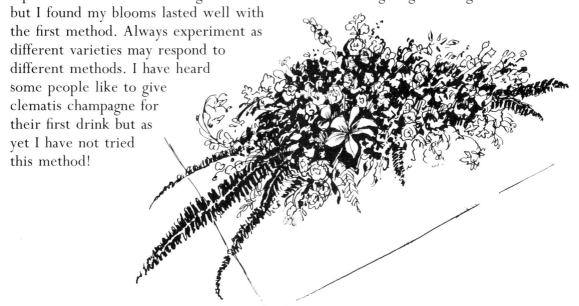

Summer flowers

This was a tea party arrangement in the home of a very special friend in Carmel Valley, California. The dainty white wire basket was ideal for the summer daisies, cow parsley 'Queen Anne's Lace', various grasses including the *Langurus ovatus* 'Hare's Tail' and, my favourite, the pods of *Raphanus raphanistrum* 'Wild Radish' (to the left and right of the basket).

Summer flowers

For the tea party I kept to a cool green and white colour scheme throughout the house. The foliage was entirely from the garden and countryside, the white border carnations and *Lilium auratum* from San Francisco Flower Market.

The container on this mantelpiece is a low cane basket fitted with a zinc lining into which I crumpled several layers of 2 in./5 cm chicken wire secured by reel wire to the basket at each side.

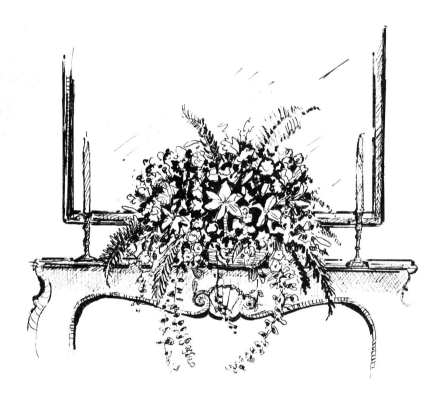

For the foliage outline I used *Dollar eucalyptus* and their seeds which cascaded beautifully in the front. In between were fronds of delicate fern. The next step was to place the border carnations within the foliage frame, finally the *Auratum lilies* for the centre area and a few of the lily buds in the intermediate area of the design.

Summer flowers

An antique carved box standing on a mahogany 'Lazy Susan' turntable which I always use when teaching so that the arrangement can be constantly turned round.

This shows the very beginning of an arrangement – five 'Soft Shield' ferns all flowing from a central point at the back of the box.

The box has a fitted zinc lining, 2 in./5 cm chicken wire well crumpled and tied down firmly with reel wire. The ferns were cut in the cool of the early morning and submerged for one hour in a bath of cold water.

Just a few flowers were eventually added to this – some pink border carnations, a centre of three deep pink *Gerberas*, three variegated *Hosta* leaves for recession. So quick and easy!

Summer flowers

A Victorian treasure of a vase which I like to arrange on the corner of the breakfast tray when I have house guests. The little boy is standing in front of a basket, and he really looks very pleased with himself when it is full of flowers! The little summer mixture is three sprays *Alcemilla mollis*, three buds and two blooms of *Rose alba* with their delicate perfume, and three stems of *Lonicera japonica* 'Aureo-reticulata'.

Summer flowers

The container is most attractive, made of porcelain to look like a woven basket with half open lid. The cherub balances on the edge with his arm lying along the side of the lid. I found it in the very North of Scotland a long time ago in the garden of a crofter's cottage. I admired it and was immediately given it as a gift. I filled it with a single summer rose and some trails of honysuckle – the perfume was delightful. It looks perfect arranged on a dressing table.

Summer flowers

A summer bedside arrangement in one of my Victorian porcelain containers –
a small bird poised on the edge of an egg. As the porcelain is very delicate the
egg has to be filled with well soaked *Oasis*. The flowers were very simple,
three buds and an open *Rosa alba* with a few sprays of the pale green *Alcemilla
mollis*.

Summer flowers

One of my most popular summer classes is 'Fruit and Flowers'. We usually use the little seedless grapes and fully opened roses to make a buffet table pyramid.

The container is a verdigris plaster dolphin holding a shell on its tail. The shell is filled with an upright block of wet *Oasis* cut to form a pyramid, this is covered with a 2 in./5 cm chicken wire cage and secured to the dolphin base with silver reel wire.

Begin by making a pretty top using a cluster of grasses or in this case *Clorophytum* plant, well washed of its earth and pinned onto the *Oasis* with small hairpins of stub wire.

About 1 lb/455 g of grapes are divided into small bunches and pinned onto the *Oasis* evenly all round. The next step is to insert the short stemmed roses deeply into the *Oasis*, again placing them all round the pyramid. The bigger the type of rose the fewer you need; usually it is necessary to have fifteen but if a small rose such as *Garnet, Carole* or *Sum* is used you would need eighteen to twenty.

Three groups of fern are arranged at the base of the shell and flowing over the rim. In between the fern I used sprays of *Vinca* to cascade downwards. Smaller pieces of *Vinca* were arranged amongst the roses and grapes. Finally the country grasses were arranged in groups of three and placed in the arrangement to give a light, dainty effect.

It is extremely important to give all the flowers, foliage and grasses a long deep conditioning drink before using in the *Oasis*. The sprays of *Vinca* should also be submerged in warm water for thirty minutes before getting their long drink.

Springtime bouquets

A white wall cherub with cornucopia was filled with three trails of ivy, three white tulips and three carnations. This was a late spring/early summer arrangement. Trails of jasmine and few beautiful white roses would look equally effective, or curving stems of honeysuckle and some creamy Roselandia roses.

Jasmine

My slight and slender jasmine-tree
That bloomest on my border tower,
Thou art more dearly loved by me
Than all the wealth of fairy bower,
I ask not while I near thee dwell,
Arabia's spice or Syria's rose;
Thy light festoons more freshly smell —
Thy virgin white more freshly glows
My mild and winsome jasmine-tree,
That climbest up the dark grey wall,
Thy tiny flowerets seem in glee
Like silver spray-drops down to fall.

Lord Morpeth

Captions to colour plates

Spring flowers

Lady with her Wheelbarrow

This beautiful collector's piece of Dutch porcelain is my favourite container. I found her in a tiny antique shop in Woodbridge, Suffolk. It was a month after we arrived back in England from Ceylon to begin our new life. First we were given a Suffolk punch horseshoe and then I found the Lady, so horseshoes do bring luck!

I usually begin a demonstration using her and she has even travelled to Paris for one of my demonstration-teaching sessions there and my audience were enchanted with her.

The wheelbarrow is fairly deep and I fill it with two strips of 2 in./5 cm of plastic coated wire netting, well crumpled and spaced, with about 2 in. above the rim of the barrow. I then tie the netting in with 28 gauge/0·38 mm silver reel wire in two places, taking the wire across the underside of the barrow.

For this cover arrangement I used a few stems of the early *Rhododendron* 'Pink Pearl' which is a shell pink with deep pink buds, three stems of jasmine, seven pale blue hyacinths, nine Pittica roses. I used foliage from my houseplants in the flat – the airy *Tremblens* fern and *Caladium* 'candidum' leaves to give interest and depth to the centre area of the arrangement.

It is important only to half fill with water a slightly sloping container, such as the wheelbarrow, then do the arrangement, preferably in the required position in the room, and finally fill to the top with water and spray with a fine mister.

Plate 1

Spring flowers

12 Solomon's Seal
 5 *Helleborus lividus ssp corsicus*
 3 *Helleborus foetidus*
 7 *Nephrolepsis* fern
 9 *Tremblens* fern
12 stems azalea
 3 leaves *Caladium* 'Candidum'

This was to be a cool spring arrangement mainly of mixed foliage and a touch of creamy yellow for an oatmeal and gold reception room. The container was a very old dimpled copper bowl with two handles, well filled with 2 in./5 cm chicken wire tied down with strong reel wire and some *Oasis* tape. I used the Solomon's Seal and the azalea as the outline or frame to the arrangement and for the centre. I saved the biggest stem of *Hellebore foetidus* and outlined this with the three beautiful *Caladium* leaves. In the intermediate areas I placed fronds of the two varieties of ferns and one or two more Solomon's Seal.

The back of this large arrangement was finished with a fan of smaller Solomon's Seal and a short stem of *Hellebore* just to hide the bare stems and the chicken wire.

Plate 2

Summer flowers

9 sprays *Nephrolepsis* fern
9 sprays *Tremblens* ferns
2 leaves *Caladium* 'Candidum'
1 spray *Hedera canariensis* 'Variegata'
5 stems *Hellebore foetidus*
1 stem *Hellebore corsicus*
5 copper-green Parrot tulips
7 stems *Lilium* 'Enchantment'
9 stems salmon antirrhinum
3 stems champagne double stock
1 stem *Lilium* 'African Queen'

This bowl was to be the centrepiece in a cream to coffee coloured room with touches of bronze and brown in cushions and carpet.

The outline of the arrangement was mainly the light touches of fern and azalea filled in with the lilies, antirrhinums and hellebores. I saved the largest lily for the focal point, edged with three *Tremblens* ferns. Well recessed to give extra depth are the two leaves of *Caladium* 'Candidum'.

I like to trail ivy, ferns and hellebores over the rim of the container and forwards to give a softening effect and to help with the feeling of depth.

The *Lilium* 'African Queen' has a slight perfume so it is a good idea to include it if possible with the other unscented lilies.

Plate 3

5

Californian episodes

My first arrangement for the demonstration was an all round massed garden mixture in shades of blue to pale and deep pink set in a beautiful stone bird bath from one of the loveliest homes in the Carmel Valley.

The 2 in./5 cm chicken wire base was well and truly anchored with several lengths of reel wire tied from side to side. In the centre of the chicken wire I placed five metal cones of graded sizes as I needed extra height at that point. The foliage which I used as the frame on the outside and at the top was the silver grey to a tinge of purple pink *Acacia bailyama purpurea*, which grows freely in the Peninsula. The main flower was the blue dwarf *Agapanthus* 'Peter Pan' and I used twenty five altogether, some smaller for the outside edges and the fuller blooms for the centre area.

To counteract the roundness of the *Agapanthus* I used twenty five stems of pinky-mauve *Francoa ramosa* which gave a soft spikiness to the design. To get the three dimensional look I used a few sprays of the very deep blue *Tibouchina urvilleana* 'Princess Flower' which was just perfect with the paler blue of *Agapanthus*.

Finally I recessed a few *Caladium* 'Candidum' leaves, added some beautiful green ferns as a contrast to the feathery acacia, allowed five stems of *Jasmin polyantum* to cascade out of three sides and two at the top of the arrangement. It was about 6 ft 5 in./1·96 m in height and 3 ft/91 cm wide.

Plate 4

Autumn flowers

A bird bath makes a very good container for a large, all round arrangement. For this arrangment I used the following:

10 stems *Stephanandra rosaceae*
 9 stems *Leucospermum cordifolium* (pin cushion protea)
 9 stems *Lilium* 'Enchantment'
 3 stems *Lilium* 'African Queen'
 7 stems *Chrysanthemum rayonanthe*
 5 stems *Cotoneaster franchetii*
 7 stems *Molucella laevis* 'Bells of Ireland'
 5 sprays *Rosa moyesii*
 3 sprays *Vitis amurensis*.

I first hammered the stems of *Stephanandra*, rose hips and proteas, then placed them in a bucket of deep water. The lilies, chrysanthemums, molucella and sprays of *Vitis amurensis* (vine) were cut at an angle (so that the stems do not lie flat in the container and can take up more water) then placed in deep water. I usually submerge vine leaves for an hour if I can as this seems to make them last well, then I give them a long drink. The conditioning drink should be at least two or three hours or, better still, all night, for arranging the following day.

My outline or frame for my design was the *Stephandra* – five points flowing out of the bird bath and three in the centre area. The remainder were added later in the intermediate area. I find cultivated *Stephandra* so beautiful as it has long graceful branches, autumnal coloured leaves and reddish stems.

Next I placed the *Lilium* 'Enchantment' evenly all round the container and two in the centre area. The three stems of *Lilium* 'African Queen' were arranged in the main part of the design as their heads are larger and deeper, therefore they are the best choice for the main eyecatching part of the arrangement.

Proteas are usually fairly short so I kept them for the centre area and to give excellent recession or depth to the whole design. The three sprays of *Vitis amurensis* (vine) were gorgeous for the finishing touches, just trailing out and over the rim of the bird bath with one spray in the centre to give continuity of colour.

Finally I filled up the container, and sprayed the whole arrangement with a fine mister. Before arranging I always place my container in the position it will finally be and half fill it with water before beginning. My chicken wire filling is always arranged several days before I need to use the container. Planning ahead is really important and saves time in the long run.

Plate 5

Autumn flowers

A simple all round arrangement for a coffee table, mantelpiece or window sill.

Seven sprays of dainty rose hips and two bunches of 'Doris' border carnations with fifteen sprays of heather which give an attractive spiky effect next to the rather round faced border carnations.

The container was a low bowl which fits neatly into a wine coaster when the arrangement is finished.

Plate 6

Autumn dried flowers

Dried flowers and foliages are ideal for a centrally heated consulting room. Arranged in a cheery colour, they add warmth to a room and this arrangement was designed for a consultant physician's rooms in Wimpole Street. I chose a frame of glycerined beech leaves to outline the arrangement. In between the beech are sprays of glycerined box. The orange *Physalis* was chosen for its colour and red *Adiantum* fern to enhance the centre area. The flat yellow heads of *Achillea* were also kept to the centre of the arrangement. There was a gold chair and pale yellow walls in the consulting room and I thought the *Achillea* would complement these. Curling wisps of grasses were added to give lightness and also five sprays of honesty. Finally three florist's wood roses were placed low and deep in the arrangement to give extra depth to the finished effect.

The back of the arrangement was finished with some short sprays of fern and box just to hide the *Oasis* and flower stems.

The container is a handsome brown tazza filled with two blocks of *Oasis* covered with 2 in./5 cm chicken wire securely tied down to the container with reel wire.

Glycerined beech was preserved in August when leaves are at their best before the sap begins to run down out of the branches. Choose really good sprays, hammer stem ends and place in a solution of $\frac{1}{3}$ glycerine to $\frac{2}{3}$ warm water. Stand stems in about 2 in./5 cm of this solution for ten days to two weeks until you see the leaves glisten and turn a golden brown colour.

Physalis, Achillea, honesty and grasses were hung in a cool dry cellar, upside down, in loose bunches from August until October.

Collect interesting seed heads and pods when you travel as they dry so well and sometimes when half open they are even more fun to use. Bark is also a good thing to look out for and collect as it mixes beautifully with autumn dried flowers in an arrangement.

Plate 7

Summer flowers

Carved camphorwood box from Ceylon

This arrangement was planned for a man's desk and the antique oriental screen made an interesting background for the garden roses.

I shall occasionally give a Recipe and Method as I do in teaching so the reader can make a similar arrangement with ease.

3 variegated *Hosta* leaves
5 stems *Berberis thunbergii atropurpurea*
3 stems *Alcemila mollis*
5 stems *Escallonia*
5 stems *Lonicera japonica Aurea reticulata*
4 Constance Spry roses
2 Josephine Bruce roses
2 Belle Blonde roses
1 Beaute rose
2 Peace roses

Arrange *Berberis* sprays from the front right-hand side of the box to the back left-hand side. Arrange the *Escallonia* sprays from the front left-hand side to the back right-hand side. Allow roses to flow through the two lanes of foliage. Place buds and smallest roses on the outside edges and largest blooms and darkest colours in the centre of the arrangement. Place the three *Hosta* leaves in the centre area to give depth and definition to the whole picture. Trails of *Lonicera* flow through the arrangement to give a soft natural look to the roses.

Plate 8

Summer bouquets

One of the prettiest brides for whom I
made a bouquet carried this handspray
of *Lilium longiflorum*. She was very
elegant, tall and slim; the bouquet
was perfect with her full skirted,
pure white wedding dress and
gorgeous floor length
veil.

I used eighteen blooms (four tight buds, nine half open and five fully open).
The lily leaves are a rich dark green colour and I picked nine of the widest
ones to use in the bouquet. It is a good idea to cut the blooms off the main
stem for their conditioning drink the day before making up. Remove all pollen
carefully as this will stain the waxy petals. Each lily is wired inside the stem
to the base of the flower with a 20 gauge/0·90 mm wire. If the lily is large,
use the heavier wire. The leaves are invisibly wired at the back with a
1 × 22 gauge/0·71 mm stub wire stitch (see diagram), then mounted onto a
20 gauge/0·90 mm 14 in./35 mm long stub wire. After wiring, cover with
white or green gutta percha. Begin making up with the buds first, followed by
the half open blooms, then to the centre area and the fully opened lilies.
Finish the lily spray with more half open blooms and finally the remaining buds
and leaves. Cut the wire handle short, about 6 in./14 cm so that it is a
comfortable length to hold. Cover this with tissue or crêpe paper and finally
with white ribbon. A neat bow at the top of the handle and behind the main
part of the bouquet is important as it gives a good finish to the back.

Summer bouquets

Lilium auratum need careful thought and planning to be incorporated into a bouquet as the heads are on the large side.

Choose varying sizes, some buds, some half open and one or two open heads for the centre. For this design I chose five *Lilium auratum* blooms, seven 'Roselandia' roses, seven stems cream freesia, fifteen sprays of lily of the valley and their own pale green leaves.

I began by arranging the smallest lily of the valley and freesias first, continuing up to the heart of the bouquet, adding the roses and then the *Auratum lilies* according to size in the centre area.

This is a truly exotic bridal mixture – White Swan roses, *Stephanotis* and lily of the valley. The perfume is fantastic and the effect of these flowers together is very beautiful. White Swan roses are fairly large and a glorious shape; only nine or ten are necessary in a curved shower with thirty stems lily of the valley and twenty pips of *Stephanotis*.

Summer bouquets

A dozen 'Roselandia' roses and a touch of lily of the valley with a few of their own leaves makes a dainty summer spray. When I use this creamy rose the effect of the shadow magnolia leaves at the back is attractive and can look beautiful against a silk or satin gown.

Summer bouquets

Suffolk was full of tall beautiful model girls! This design was specially planned for just such a bride. Twelve white Virgo roses, thirty stems lily of the valley, thirty pips of *Stephanotis*. I used lily of the valley leaves and a few rose leaves near the centre area. The wiring of this bouquet was covered with strips of silver paper, not gutta percha – the effect is fairylike, though it may sound a little strange!

Summer bouquets

A small bride asked me to design a special bouquet for her but she insisted she wanted *Longiflorum lilies*! It seemed a problem as the lilies are large, but with the help of waterproof lace ribbon I made this posy-shaped design using five sprays of variegated ivy and in the centre three sprays of variegated *Euonymus*.

Longiflorum lilies are one of my favourite flowers and in my Ceylon garden they grew to 6 ft/1·8 m and produced beautiful heads of ten to twelve blooms. I used them extensively in arrangements and for weddings.

Many people ask for a single lily sheaf which is extremely easy to make and effective. If, however, a girl wants originality, what could be better than including the other two bride's favourite flowers, lily of the valley and *Stephanotis*? A curving shower bouquet with lily of the valley on the outside edges and a touch in the centre, *Stephanotis* running through from the outside to the centre where the *Longiflorum lilies* are placed, with three fronds of ladder fern and a touch of variegated *Euonymus*, plus the lily of the valley leaves.

Summer bouquets

In warm climates such as California, Ceylon, South Africa and the Middle East carnations are a boon. In Paris they are also a well loved flower and I find I am always asked to include a carnation arrangement when I work in France. Lily of the valley is not always easy to obtain, but in the hot climate areas one can always look out for tiny *Dendrobium* orchids to use to give the dainty effect which lilies give. In these bouquets I used the leaves of lily of the valley and variegated *Euonymus* sprays near the centre of each posy.

I usually wire carnations with a 2 × 22/0·71 mm gauge, 14 in./35 cm long stub wire or a 1 − 20/0·90 mm gauge 14 in./35 cm long stub wire. The calyx is pierced with the stub wire and this is secured with silver reel wire across the calyx and down the flower stem and stub wire.

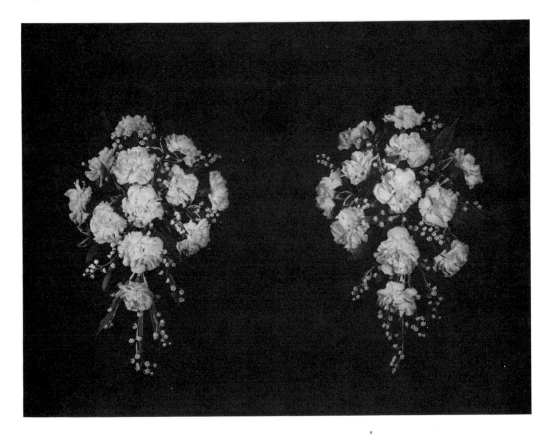

Carnation

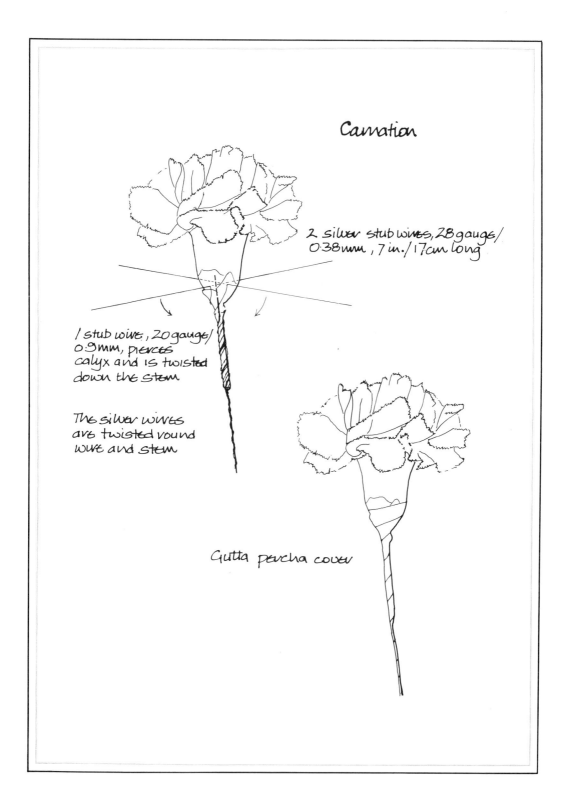

2 silver stub wires, 28 gauge/ 0·38mm, 7 in./17cm long

1 stub wire, 20 gauge/ 0·9mm, pierces calyx and is twisted down the stem

The silver wires are twisted round wire and stem

Gutta percha cover

Summer bouquets

Petite girls need equally petite feminine flowers and this was a bouquet which I dreamed up for just such a bride: two white *Catteleya* orchids with a pale yellow throat and thirty stems of lily of the valley plus their own pale green foliage. *Phalaenopsis* orchids look equally delightful for this design.

Orchids are carefully wired with a 22 gauge/0·71 mm stub wire 14 in./35 cm long into the stem and secured with fine silver reel wire. Wire stems are covered with gutta percha.

Summer bouquets

This was a design which I loved to make in Ceylon as there were endless colours of *Gerbera* in the garden. The hyacinths were impossible to grow there but I used agapanthus pipped instead. The carnations are feathered. This means the petals are taken from the flower and re-grouped into dainty groups of two or three petals wired with the finest silver reel wire. They are then covered with gutta percha and mounted into groups of three on a 22 gauge/0·71 mm stub wire. The pipped hyacinths are also wired into groups of three onto a 22 gauge/0·71 mm stub wire and covered with gutta percha.

Gerberas have a 22 gauge/0·71 mm stub wire pushed into the stem which is then secured with reel wire across the stem and down the stub wire.

Variegated ivy leaves give a delicate effect in the centre area of the *Gerbera* bouquet.

Californian episodes

Each summer I cross the ocean to California, where in certain areas life seems similar to my old life in Ceylon. Tropical flowers grow profusely plus many other varieties, and the wild flowers are unbelievably beautiful.

My first stop is usually San Francisco and a visit to the Flower Market. It is a fairly small area but everything a flower arranger needs is there. One has to have a trade pass in order to purchase flowers and sundries, and this is the general rule in other world flower markets. My Californian interior design friends help search out the special flowers and sundries which we need and the market men laugh at the English names for stub wire, reel wire and tubes! Their words are completely different.

We then set off south to the country where friends gather each year to arrange flowers with me. We usually work in the gardens or by the swimming pool and as we arrange the humming birds fly past us towards the fuschias which they love. The scene is a little paradise, with the very blue sky, sunshine *ad lib* and clear champagne air.

My approach to flower arranging in California is slightly different from that in England. I am lucky to have the gardens of friends from which to pick flowers so I am inspired by the materials available in each garden. I still plan a colour scheme for each room which I am going to decorate, to complement the colours in a carpet perhaps or a painting or cushions. It is also important to know whether the occasion is formal or informal and which containers are available to use.

Then the cutting begins early in the morning. All materials are conditioned and left standing in deep buckets of water out of any draughts. At this stage I usually draw some rough sketches of the arrangements, writing alongside the number of flowers and foliages which I would like to use.

It is important to cut very carefully so that a precious plant is not left in a bad shape. One can often cut side shoots from larkspur and delphinium, leaving the main stem untouched in the border – the same applies to cutting foliage. It is

of course easier for someone who has been gardening for many years, but if in doubt one should always ask the gardener or lady of the house.

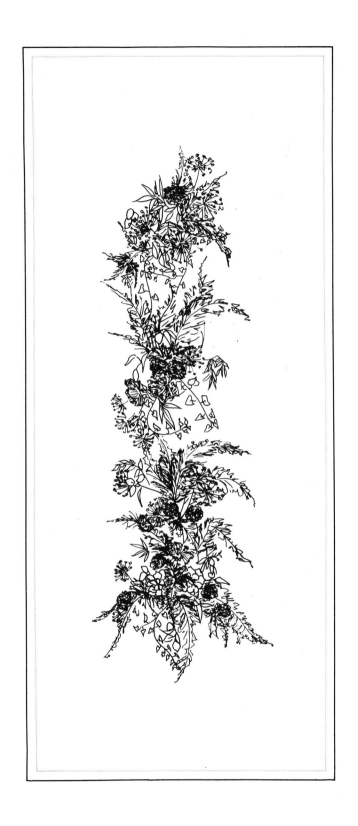

Californian episodes

A tea-party was given in my honour to which seventy guests were invited from Monterey, Carmel and San Francisco.

Out came my sketch book to plan arrangements round the house. The first was a fountain as one entered the front door. My colour scheme was green and gold. The fountain was made of a redwood pole secured in a plant pot of plaster of paris. At intervals of 18 in./45 cm a cat-food tin was nailed onto the pole and the top one was fixed on the very end of the pole. Each tin was filled with wet *Oasis*.

I used eighteen long ferns and six smaller ones at the top and about the same amount of wild fennel which has a light lacy look. For the golden look we cut marigolds which were plentiful, growing below the rose bushes in the garden and for recession I used the 'Hens and Chickens' as they are called in California – *Sempervirens tectorum*. Also included in the design were stems of green and ripe lemons. This arrangment lasted well for four weeks with only an occasional addition of a marigold or two. I topped up with water and sprayed twice daily, which is a must of course.

The ferns which I used were very varied. I used them all frequently as I used to do in Ceylon – finding them light and dainty in arrangements. All should be cut at dawn if possible, submerged in a bath of water for an hour, then given a long deep drink. The main varieties which I was cutting all the time were *Nephrolepsis exaltata* 'Sword Fern' *Cyrtomium falcatum* 'Holly Fern', *Polystichum Setiferum* 'Soft Shield Fern' and Leather fern – very hardy and plentiful – which can be bought in Covent Garden. It is imported from France.

It is interesting to note that the wild fennel is known as 'Sweet Anise'; the smell of the cut stem is of aniseed and it is sometimes used in cooking, as it is a herb.

Californian episodes

The second of my entrance arrangements in the same green and gold colour scheme showed off the beautiful ferns which contrasted well against the pale wall in the background. In between the ferns I used fennel to give a light lacy effect. Sprays of lemon came cascading out over the rim of the container and up into the heart of the arrangement. Once again the gold marigolds came into their own in the centre area of the design and two *Sempervirens tectorum* were perfect for recession. Below the mirror by the arrangments there lies a beautiful Chinese plate into which I placed a perfect, ripe lemon.

The container was a rather special rosewood bowl set on a three-legged Chinese stand, with a pyrex centre filled with crumpled chicken wire which was tied securely with 28 gauge/0·38 mm reel wire at each end.

Californian episodes

I crumpled 2 in./5 cm chicken wire into a low oblong dish, secured with 28 gauge/0·38 mm reel wire. The arrangement was to be kept low and would be reflected in the mirror, also the old Chinese plate.

To give a lightness to the design I used five sprays of the attractive *Hedera helix* 'Goldheart' at each end and in the centre I used two *Sempervirens tectorum* to give definition. In the intermediate areas I used three sprays of lemon, a touch of leather fern and some maidenhair fern. I found two fronds of rust coloured leather fern which picked up the colour in the plate and also the rust colour of the Goldheart ivy stems which gave added interest.

Californian episodes

My hanging arrangement in the Turkish curd pot is filled with 2 in./5 cm chicken wire well crumpled into the base and coming up above the rim. It is secured with silver reel wire tied round the chicken wire and attached to each chain at the side of the curd pot. I used five trails of *Vinca major* 'Variegata', five trails of *Jasmin polyanthum* and five blooms of the deciduous clematis with lavender coloured blooms and touches of *Thalictrum T dipterocarpum* 'Meadow Rue' lavender, which is also pale mauve and has very dainty flowers all the way up the stem.
These curd pots are hung round the camel's neck with milk in them and with the swaying to and fro the milk turns to curds, or so they say!

Californian episodes

The Monterey County Committee of The Guide Dogs for Blind Inc invited me to give a demonstration in the summer before an audience of five hundred in the Steinbeck Forum of the Monterey Conference Center. I undertook the request but cancelled all other teaching and social engagements for the week preceding the demonstration. Such is the preparation beforehand, one really has to be highly organised from start to finish and take care of the tiniest detail in order to make the whole project a great success.

First we visited the Steinbeck Forum to see the stage which was really huge and was going to be splendid for working on. My sketch book came out and I sketched plant groups for each end of the stage and was able to borrow houseplants from a nursery garden in Monterey and also some attractive basket containers for displaying the plants.

My friends were fantastic and rallied round to help. We cut from four beautiful gardens in the Peninsula and from the countryside so that all my arrangements would look very natural and informal. My plan was to do seven arrangements and three jasmin ribbons for a cake table, all in two hours! Everything went according to plan from start to finish and we made $5,000 for The Guide Dogs for the Blind, enough to buy a complete Man Dog Unit, which was marvellous.

When giving demonstrations timing is all important. My plans for this demonstration began in London six months ahead of schedule, the cake cloth was made and details of table size sent to California. My copper Turkish containers were all sent off by sea.

The week prior to the demonstration visits were made to the four gardens to see what would be available. I also made a trip to a local carnation nursery to order spray carnations.

The day before the demonstration all the cutting and conditioning of flowers was carried out, the stage plants arranged in position and all the containers taken to the stage.

Californian episodes

On the day of the demonstration there was a very early rise plus getting all the flowers and foliage down to the Steinbeck Center.

My plan for speed of work is to have a long table on which to arrange and a 'Lazy Susan' turntable. If bamboo matting is available the work table is covered with this as it lends itself to flowerwork – we managed to find some in San Francisco. Behind me there was another long table with my containers placed in order of use, plus flowers and foliage to be used with each different container. My scissors, sprayer, tubes, reel wire were all in an attractive low basket on the main table.

My opening speech was very brief, light and happy. And then straight down to work – there was little time to spare for talk without work. As my arranging took shape I explained why and how I was doing various things. My audience asked questions too, which was good.

As each arrangement was finished, I placed it on a special stand at the correct height; for this I have a range of bamboo stands and pedestals. At the end it is important to invite the audience onto the stage to look into the arrangements and again ask questions.

My cake top was arranged in a very old silver container which was about the size of a very dainty tea cup. The flowers consisted of tiny trails of *Jasmin polyanthum*, pale pink Cécile Brunner roses, and *Adiantum cuneatum* or maidenhair fern.

At each side of the table I arranged curving trails of jasmine finished in the centre with pale pink gauze ribbon bows. The ribbon was bought in France and it is wired along the edge with a very fine reel wire so remaining beautifully crisp.

The cloth was specially made in London for the demonstration and consisted of a stiff petticoat or lining with a Swiss voile top cover reaching to the floor, but cut in the shape of petals. A second short top was also cut in petals and fitted the table top exactly. The effect was very bridal and feminine.

Californian episodes

This could be a winter decoration but it was in fact finished with marguerites, sprays of *Raphanus raphanistrum* 'Wild Radish' and a few small *Caladium* 'Candidum' leaves — all very summery.

The plant pot was filled with plaster of paris and the Californian oak branch (all one piece) from the Monterey woods was placed in the centre to set.

The next step was to fix the wet *Oasis* rounds with chicken wire cages onto two different levels of the branch. Care has to be taken when inserting the flowers as the *Oasis* is fairly delicate. The final touch was a stem or two of shiny green ivy and reindeer moss to cover the plaster of paris. Notice the whiskery Spanish moss growing on the branch; this grows all over the oaks in the Peninsula and is typical of the scene.

Californian episodes

7 trails *Jasmin polyanthemus*
20 pink roses, Cécile Brunner
15 stems border Carnations
3 small *Caladium* 'Candidum' leaves
for large candlestick
3 *Begonia rex* leaves
for small candlestick
20 stems *Adiantum cuncatum*

The larger of the two candlesticks was 4 ft/1·2 m tall and the candle was a cathedral candle – extremely long, very elegant and incredibly difficult to find. Shops seem reluctant to stock them. The smaller candlestick was the normal height, very old and made of brass.

In each case I used a candlecup with wet *Oasis* covered with chicken wire and secured with reel wire to the base of the cup. The candles are then inserted into a plastic candleholder which is fixed into the centre of the *Oasis*.

Flowers are arranged evenly all round with the trails of jasmin cascading downwards towards the table. Place largest roses in the centre part of the cup and recess some by cutting them quite short.

The maidenhair fern gives a fine edge or frame to the flowers, looks ideal as it is so dainty, but must be kept sprayed with a fine mister otherwise it will die quite quickly. Always have extra cut and kept in a cool place for replacements.

Californian episodes

A candlecup arrangement is ideal for a dinner party when you have little room to spare for the flowers, as they are lifted up and off the table.

The cups are obtainable in all flower shops and are sold in silver, gold, black or white plastic. The cup fits neatly into a candlestick.

Method
Soak *Oasis* foam (this can be bought to fit the cup) until thoroughly wet, place in cup, then make a small chicken wire cage to anchor the *Oasis*, tie the wire cage to the candlecup with 28 gauge/0·38 mm reel wire. Do not tie the cup onto the candlestick as you will need to pick the cup up and take to the sink for spraying daily.

Place a candle in the centre of the *Oasis*.

Flowers
It is very important to condition them well before using in *Oasis* in a small container such as a candlecup. Collect or buy dainty foliage and flowers, such as variegated ivy, *Vinca major* 'Variegata', jasmine, small roses or border carnations. All the flowers in the photograph were cut from the garden in the cool of the evening and had a long deep drink all night. I submerged the *Euonymus* for a good hour as soon as I picked it, then stood it upright for a conditioning drink. First I arranged the five sprays of *Euonymus* in the *Oasis*, three stems cascading downward and two very close to the candle area. My ten Cécile Brunner went in next, evenly all round, with the bigger blooms cut shorter and placed in the centre area.

I managed to cut some very pretty pink fuchsias to combine with the roses as the arrangment was mainly shades of pink. These last extremely well with a long deep drink beforehand.

Seven miniature daisies were added to each side, two miniature heads of hydrangea cut short and placed to give recession.

A touch of wild radish was added, and a few fronds of leather fern to give a deep green shade thus contrasting well with the pale green *Euonymus* and wild radish.

Finally spray with a fine mister; this is most important for candlecup arrangements as the flowers do get warm from the candle-flame and diners around them.

Try to choose a scented flower if possible to include in your dinner table arrangements as it is specially nice to sit down and inhale the delicate perfume. The Cécile Brunner which I used has a delicious perfume, not too strong, and would combine beautifully with my favourite *Jasmin polyanthemus*, as both have pink buds with flowers turning to white.

Californian episodes

The container is original, very old, and made in China. From a distance it looks like a dark brown jar but in fact it is entirely woven with very fine cane. Inside is a plastic container which fits exactly. I filled this with 2 in./5 cm chicken wire tied down securely with 28 gauge/0·38 mm reel wire.

It is ideal for a light informal breakfast room arrangement and I used shades of pink flowers to tone with the mauve to pink tiles on which the flowers were to be placed.

The materials gathered from the garden were three very curving stems of rosemary, three dainty cascades of jasmine, three sprays of *Thalictrum*, seven pink roses, three small heads of pink hydrangea.

If you have the luck to find a superb mixture like this in the garden they will arrange themselves in your container – they are so attractive that they do the work for you!

Californian episodes

M. LANSDOWNE

This arrangement of mixed pink flowers was cut entirely from the garden of my friend in Carmel Valley, California. It was an all round posy of mainly oleander 'Rose Bay'. The outline foliage was the blue-grey *Acacia bailyana purpurea*. I used three stems of a beautiful hollyhock from the cutting garden, also some deep pink single stock and a few stems of *Dianthus*. The container was a shell pink low dish filled with 2 in./5 cm chicken wire and tied down with silver reel wire.

All the flowers were cut early in the morning and placed in deep water for a few hours. The stems of oleander were slit and placed in warm water. This quickly stops the latex from escaping. They can also be dipped into boiling water for a second and then given a deep, long drink. I like to remove a great many leaves as this gives a lightness to the blossom. It must be remembered that the shrub is POISONOUS so care must be taken if children are assisting.

This arrangement was for a very feminine pink and white bedroom to go on the dressing table and be reflected in the mirrors.

Californian episodes

A hamper basket is one of the most popular containers with all my students. The lid can be left wide open or only half open if flowers are scarce and a smaller arrangement is necessary. This basket has a fitted tin lining into which the student has crumpled several layers of 2 in./5 cm chicken wire and tied this down at each side of the basket with a short length of reel wire.

The foliage frame is the dark green leather fern which grows so well in California and other warm climates. It made an excellent background to the pale yellow wild fennel.

To the left of the basket is the attractive wild radish, *Raphanus raphanistrum*. This grows in huge clumps with long stems and the pale green pods grow all the way down the stems. One sees these clumps very often lying flattened on the ground by the weight of the many pods.

This arrangement was mostly wild flowers with a very few garden flowers — ideal for an informal occasion.

Californian episodes

This is a magnificent flower arranging scene next to the Pacific Ocean on the Monterey Peninsula, where everyone has brought their basket to the class to fill with wild flowers and garden treasures. First I demonstrated a basket arrangement and then everyone arranged her own using the flowers of her choice. First the containers were filled with 2 in./5 cm chicken wire well crumpled and tied to the cane of the basket with a small piece of silver wire at each side. Then the containers were half filled with water and each person begins with a foliage outline, filling in with flowers in the centre. Two or three larger flowers were chosen and placed in the centre of the basket and gradually smaller, daintier flowers were added, radiating outwards without the stems crossing.

The climate in the Monterey Peninsula is very like that of up-country Ceylon amongst the tea. The same mists prevail and many flowers and shrubs are indentical, thriving in the coolness of the atmosphere. I feel incredibly at home in this part of the world.

Californian episodes

A needlework basket with a silk finish to the lid was filled with a waterproof zinc lining. Well crumpled 2 in./5 cm chicken wire was tied down with reel wire. It is a good example of a student's start to her arrangement – three daisies with a frame of maidenhair fern as the outline. I like to submerge the maidenhair fern in a bath of cold water for a soak of one hour before gently hammering the stems and placing them in deep water.

Californian episodes

A glass pyrex dish makes an excellent container for a long low table arrangement. I usually place a pinholder in the bottom of the dish with well crumpled chicken wire layered on top and about 1 in./2·5 cm above the rim of the dish. Tie chicken wire in securely with silver reel wire from one side under the dish and across to the other side or use oasis tape before the water is poured in, otherwise the tape will not stick to the glass edge.

When the arrangement is complete I like to put the pyrex into a silver entrée dish and it really is interesting to see the gleam of silver through the flower arrangement.

Californian episodes

In California and in many other warm climates such as Bermuda, the South of France and Greece, container planting is extremely popular. The line drawing opposite shows what an attractive effect can be achieved in a small area.

In the background you see a gazebo with hanging baskets of petunias and geraniums. In the foreground are tiers of low, wide clay pots filled with massed zinnias, marigolds, phlox and geraniums, a true feast of colour.

In London this is an excellent idea for our small roof gardens and patios as you can keep each container constantly full of colour from spring into late autumn.

It is necessary to have good drainage in the bottom of the containers – use stones or broken clay pots, fill with an earth and compost mixture ready to plant the seedlings. If you buy larger plants, place these into the container, then add your soil and press plants firmly down – water well and shade until they are established. In Ceylon we used to shade all newly planted cuttings and/or plants with bracken or fern.

Ceylon magic

The setting was in a beautiful valley known as Dimbula and the club, called Radella, set amongst hills of dark green tea bushes 5,500 ft/1067 m above sea level. The Planters Association of Ceylon were to celebrate their centenary year with a special party on 17 April 1954. Her Majesty The Queen and Prince Philip were to be the special guests, as they were staying nearby, resting, in Nuwara Eliya on their World Tour.

I was asked to organise and carry out the flower arrangments for the party. First I chose a team of helpers, talented friends from up-country. We had many meetings to discuss my ideas, make plans and get organised. We all guarded our special flowers which we were going to use; it was quite difficult as we had the monsoon to contend with and this usually did an incredible amount of damage to our up-country gardens. Orchids, for instance, had to be covered with tiny metal umbrellas to keep them from being spotted by raindrops.

My plan was to use only flowers found in Ceylon, so the theme was definitely tropical. The presentation basket which I arranged for The Queen was a mixture of orchids, mainly *Cymbidiums*, in shades of cream to gold with pale green ferns including maidenhair, running through to soften the orchids. I added green 'bun moss' to finish, this gave some recession and covered any sign of chicken wire. The basket was a very pretty shape, locally made and lined with zinc so I was able to moisten the moss and we hoped The Queen would take it to her yacht Britannia and sail away across the Indian Ocean with it!

None of us knew the colour of The Queen's dress so it was a stroke of luck that she wore a primrose coloured outfit and so the orchids toned beautifully with her coat.

The royal dais flowers were three colossal floor to ceiling arrangements of pale pink to deep pink flowers and silver foliages. We used long sprays of *Congea*, pale and deep pink carnations, pale pink to very deep pink *Anthurium*, *Alpinia nutans* 'Shell Ginger' and *Phaeomeria magnifica* 'Torch Ginger'. These ginger plants are truly magnificent for large arrangements, the flowers are very

Ceylon magic

long lasting and waxy looking. The leaves are heavy and have to be stripped away as they conceal the beauty of the flowers, and other more attractive leaves were substituted. The main foliage which we used were dainty tree fern, silvery acacia and a feathery type of bamboo plus shorter silver foliage such as *Seneciogreyii*, *Senecio maritime*, rue and rosemary for recession. We also used some of the smaller *Anthurium* leaves as they are such a well-defined shape.

At the front of the dais were arranged several hanging baskets; again these were locally made of Sinhalese cane with zinc linings which we filled with crumpled chicken wire and damp moss. We had cascades of pink *Antigonan leptopus* 'Coral Vine' flowing out of these arrangements with tiny *Anthuriums*, sprays of pink orchids and maidenhair fern.

When The Queen and Prince Philip walked up the steps to the dais from the garden below it was almost dusk, so I had planned with the electricians to have each arrangement lit with a pink bulb from the very centre; this was very effective and much admired.

It was interesting that all the magnificent long lasting tropical flowers which we had treasured and used, all continued on to Kandy for yet another special party to be held for Her Majesty and Prince Philip. The main reason for their lasting was of course that we had conditioned every stem before use; they were picked early in the morning, stems slit, leaves removed and left in deep buckets of water all day, before packing in the evening for dispatching to the Club next day.

We had all experimented months beforehand with our flowers, trying various ideas on conditioning such as aspirin and various crystals which were said to be beneficial but in the long run we found the best method of all was simply cutting in the cool of the evening and giving them a long deep drink. Only the *Antigonan* and the *Petrea* were given sugar water. All the ferns and silvery *Senecios* were submerged in baths of water for one hour before being placed upright for their long drink.

Autumn *flowers*

10 stems *Vinca major* 'Variegata'
5 stems blackberries
7 stems *Chincherinchees*
10 stems white anemones
3 large variegated ivy leaves

This was a table centre in green and white for a luncheon party. I like to float the *Vinca* underwater for an hour before standing upright for the conditioning drink, as it will then last far longer.

The low bowl was filled with 2 in./5 cm chicken wire well crumpled, then secured with reel wire from side to side.

The flowers radiated outwards from a central point so that none of the stems crossed each other. The largest of the anemone blooms were placed in the centre part of the design with the smaller flowers and buds radiating outwards to join stems of daintier *Chincherinchees, Vinca* and blackberries. The three ivy leaves were added last giving recession and covering areas of visible chicken wire.

Autumn flowers

My last arrangement of the year was an informal country mixture for Her Majesty The Queen, commissioned by a friend.

The dish was a white oval one about 2 in./5 cm deep. Chicken wire was well crumpled to give several layers from bottom to just above the rim level, secured with 28 gauge/0·38 mm reel wire.

The scheme was green and white as the white Jack Frost rose was available in the market, three beautiful white hyacinths featured in the centre area and all the foliages came from a Sussex garden and they included *Vinca major* 'Variegata', grey green *Garrya elliptica cathian*, a touch of *Senecio greyii* and a few racemes of creamy yellow *Mahonia japonica*. *Vinca* lasts well if stem ends are dipped into boiling water and then submerged completely in a bowl of slightly warm water.

A natural arrangement of border carnations, hydrangea heads, ferns and grasses, with caladium leaves for recession, in a copper Turkish kettle.

Autumn flowers

A copper hot water bottle was the oldest type of bed warmer. This one was lent to me to arrange an interesting mixture of five sprays of wild clematis 'Old Man's Beard', three curving stems of driftwood collected from the banks of the River Orwell in Suffolk, a bunch of luscious pale green grapes (to match the flower of the wild clematis) and lastly five sprays of variegated ivy.

I fixed crumpled 2 in./5 cm chicken wire into the container and this was held in place by the rim of the copper container. The driftwood went neatly into the chicken wire and the rest of the material flowed prettily out of the quite small opening. This left only the bunch of grapes to be fixed with 2 × 22 gauge/0·71 mm, 14 in./35 cm long wires across the base of the bunch and finally secured into the chicken wire.

Flower Arrangement
by
MARY ADAMS
13 15, St. Stephen's Lane

Autumn plant arrangements

A mixed plant group in a London hotel. The occasion was a demonstration which I gave as a flower arrangement promotion scheme to which all my past and present students were invited and asked to bring their friends.

In the background, standing in a large basket container was a Kentia palm in front of which was a *Diffenbachia picta roehrsii* and a *Dracaena deremensis*, both set in pretty Chinese baskets with lids attached and at an angle.

On the left the cherub bird bath was filled with maidenhair and *Tremblens* ferns massed and the pots hidden with green bun moss to give depth to the centre.

Another fern group was placed very low indeed with a *Diffenbachia picta Bausei* coming forwards out of the fern group – all were massed in a low copper dish. Two attractive 'rocks' which light up can be seen to the left of the plant group. These are ideal for a small patio where perhaps steps need a glimmer of light at night.

All the plants were sprayed regularly which keeps a moist atmosphere around them. Plants like to be grouped and seem to thrive in this way – ferns prefer a room with early morning sunlight and they need watering almost every day in the summer. Most plants are sold with excellent care cards and if these instructions are read and followed they will last for a very long time.

Autumn plant arrangements

It is important to have a mixture of house plants in the home as they make the atmosphere healthy, quite apart from being restful to the eyes and soul. Also they are always there, filling a beautiful container and making a natural picture in a room.

Autumn dried flowers

In our Suffolk house we had a large, dry, airy cellar which was ideal for preserving all my dried materials. The flowers were cut when they were in perfect condition, not quite fully out and hung in loose bunches of ten stems upside down from a beam. *Achillae*, golden rod, larkspur, delphinium, honesty, statice, were a few of the successful ones. I experimented each year with new varieties. It was a novel idea for me as in Ceylon we had such an abundance of flowers and foliage that preserving was unnecessary.

August and September are the best months to cut foliage for preserving in glycerine, before the sap begins to leave the branches. My favourite is beech as it turns to such a beautiful shade of pale brown but oak, sweet chestnut, eucalyptus and box are equally successful, all turning to a slightly different shade which is interesting. Use very warm water to add to the glycerine; two parts water to one part glycerine is really the best proportion.

Hammer the stem ends and stand in the glycerine solution immediately. It does not have to be very deep, 2–4 in./5–10 cm is sufficient, but it is necessary to top up at the end of a week with more of the solution. Usually the glycerine has reached the topmost leaf by the fifth day but the branches must be kept in the solution for at least ten days to two weeks, sometimes much longer for heavier, larger leaves such as laurel. Preserve only really perfect sprays of leaves – many are found to be eaten by insects.

Autumn dried flowers

Hydrangea heads can also be preserved in glycerine but another successful method is just to stand them in cold water until they gradually dry completely, thus retaining their colour. *Molucella* can be treated by the two methods, in glycerine they turn brown, in water they dry and become a pale honey shade.

Roses, gentians, zinnias and many other summer flowers can be preserved in silica gel. Spread a layer of silica gel in the bottom of a tin or box then place the flowers face upwards, cover with more silica gel pouring into the petals and around the flower face, continue in this way until the box is full, cover with a tight lid and leave for four or five days. Great care must be taken when the flowers come out of the powder as they are very brittle. It is really great fun experimenting with different flowers from year to year. It is so interesting to keep a few of the precious summer flowers all through winter by this method and the colours really do remain bright.

Ferns, when mature, can be pressed with great success, also bracken. The method which I found most successful in Suffolk was to place the fronds in between sheets of newspaper which were then weighted down with spare boards which we had for shelving, etc (again I used our airy dry cellar for this). The pressing could also be carried out under a carpet but do not hoover over the spot as the fern will be ruined. The drying process is lengthy and takes eight to ten weeks but it is rewarding; the fern remains a lovely pale green colour and the bracken turns to pale honey. Small fronds of fern can be pressed in between sheets of blotting paper or in a spare magazine.

Autumn dried flowers

Try to find beautiful logs when walking in country woods. They make such attractive containers for dried flower arrangements and fit well into a fireplace during the summer. This log had a superb hole in the centre into which I sank a block of *Oasis* covered with a cage of chicken wire and tied down with 28 gauge/0·38 mm black reel wire.

The beautiful fronds of pale green *Osmunda* ferns made an excellent frame for a few centre flowers, so the arrangement was really very economical. The colour scheme was pale green, creamy yellow through to gold and orange. The cream through to yellow flowers were dried *Achillea*, the gold to orange flowers were *Physalis* and in the very centre two dried heads of South African *Protea* which were coffee coloured. For recession I added some really short *Helichrysum* in cream and gold. Any areas of *Oasis* showing were covered finally by some dry reindeer moss pinned into the *Oasis* with hair pins of 22 in. × 7 in./55 cm × 18 cm stub wire.

Christmas workshop

Buffet table decoration

Fresh materials
1 branch *Cedrus atlantica glauca Beissn* 'Blue Cedar'
1 branch variegated holly
5 stems *Thuja* 'Aureospicata'
Dried materials
5 stems larch with cones
5 graded fir cones (medium to large)

Method
It is necessary to divide the large branch of 'Blue Cedar' into two long
8 in./20 cm pieces for each end and two shorter pieces 4 in./10 cm for each
side. The remaining pieces can be kept carefully to one side to add later in the
design. Remove pine needles from the end of the stem to make it slimmer for
insertion into the oasis at each end and each side. A striking effect can be
achieved by letting the holly sprays flow from the top end of the arrangement
through the centre and across diagonally to the opposite end.

The larch branches can do the same, flowing diagonally across in the other
direction.

Try to collect variegated holly with berries if possible. If there are no berries,
artificial and very real looking berries can be bought at the flower shop. These
are sold in bunches of fifty and can easily be twisted round the holly stems to
look natural.

The golden *Thuja* looks extremely attractive in the central area of the
arrangement. Two pieces should be kept fairly low at each side and the other
three pieces raised in the intermediate areas and one close to the candle.

The five pine cones can be given a wire 'stem' by taking a long 14 in./35 cm
stub wire, 22 gauge/0·71 mm and carefully slipping this under the pine seed
scales encircling the entire cone. When the wire meets, twist it together to
form a double leg which is inserted into the *Oasis*.

106

Christmas workshop

The cones should be kept near the centre of the design as they are heavy looking and make a good eyecatching area. It is a good idea to have the fir cones also diagonally placed, perhaps in a group of two to one side and three diagonally opposite. To balance this we very often make small red ribbon bows to be placed on the opposite sides of the design but this is left to the individual as many of my students are not ribbon inclined.

My Christmas Workshop is usually held in a private studio and this time it was in Kinnerton Street SW1. Each student shared a large table as one tends to need a big work area for Christmas table arrangements. The materials used were all fresh except for very real looking waxed Christmas roses.

Christmas workshop

In the first photograph can be seen the plastic base and a block of *Oasis*. This was covered with a 2 in./5 cm chicken wire cage and fixed to the base with *Oasis*-fix tape. In the centre is a plastic candle holder into which goes the tall red Christmas candle.

All flower shops stock these sundries all the year round and most will sell candles and ribbons if requested.

Equipment for the flower room

Equipment for the flower room

Collect your equipment gradually so that it is not too big an outlay at the beginning.

Scissors, secateurs and chicken wire, 28 gauge/0·38 mm silver reel wire, a long spouted can and a fine mister are all the important items to buy for immediate use.

Later, collect tubes for giving extra height, pinholders, *Oasis* and, of course, all your containers. This will take time and it is good to have inexpensive baskets, modern containers and antiques.

As well as investing in the ordinary 2 in./5 cm chicken wire, buy some plastic coated wire for your silver containers or perhaps for porcelain and glass containers. It is available in green and white.

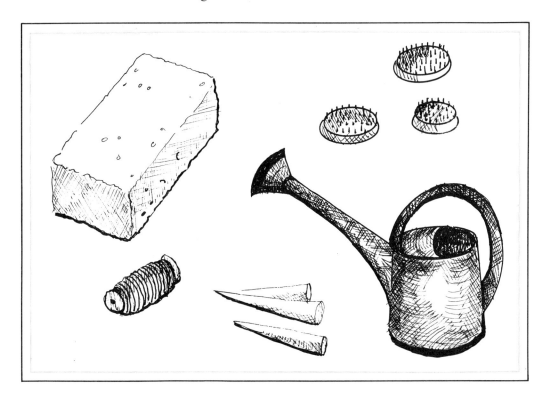

Equipment for the flower room

Oasis Tape (for securing chicken wire to container), *Oasis Fix* (for securing underside of pinholder to base of the container, for extra strength). These two items are very useful aids to have at hand.

As well as being on the look out for attractive containers, it is a good idea to seek out a variety of stands and pedestals for showing your flower arrangements off to advantage. There are some extremely pretty bamboo stands available and I could not be without the mahogany pedestal I found in Framlingham, Suffolk, on one of our 'antique searching' outings.

The roughly woven rush basket is almost a must for the flower room. It lends itself so well to the natural style of flower arranging. It is available in a tiny size, graduating up to washing-up bowl size! It looks delightful filled with plants, enchanting arranged with flowers and herbs in summer, and perfect with daffodils in the spring. A container for all seasons in fact, and one of the most popular in my series of flower arrangement classes.

I think a turntable is most useful to have for your flower arranging. There are the cheaper plastic ones (for cake making) to be bought in kitchen equipment shops. Then there are the antique ones made in mahogany or oak, found in antique shops. These are becoming increasingly rare.

Equipment for the flower room

If you are experimenting with bouquets you will need a good range of florist's wires and these can be bought from your flower shop.

Stub wires are available as follows:
30 gauge/0·32 mm × 7 in./18 cm and 32 gauge/0·28 mm × 7 in./18 cm.

These are known as rose wires and are used for wiring down violets and snowdrops, and for securing and pinning roses. They are also used for wiring rose leaves and carnation grass.

24 gauge/0·56 mm × 7 in./18 cm for wiring slightly heavier flowers, such as narcissi and palma violets.

22 gauge/0·71 mm × 7 in./18 cm, 12 in./30 cm and 14 in./35 cm for foundation work on wreaths and for mounting flowers for bouquet work such as tulips, roses or carnations.

20 gauge/0·90 mm × 7 in./18 cm, 12 in./30 cm, 14 in./35 cm for heavy flowers, such as gladiolii and delphiniums, and for mounting flowers for wreath work.

All wires are sold by weight and are sold in packets of 8 lb/455 g.

Reels of silver wire and black wire are made in various gauges from 24 gauge/ 0·56 mm to 32 gauge/0·28 mm. The finest, 32 gauge/0·28 mm, is for wiring lily of the valley and freesias. The 30 gauge/0·32 mm is usually used for sweet peas and some ferns.

Gutta percha or Gutta Tape are also necessary. This is used to bind the wire stems of the flower and gives a smooth finish. It is sold in boxes of five flat reels and is available in white, green and brown; most flower shops will sell it to you but as it is workroom equipment it is advisable to order the amount needed ahead of time.

Containers

Copper and brass are ideal for setting off flowers and plants. Collect them whenever you see attractive shapes. My collection is varied, and they come from Ceylon, Suffolk, Turkey and India. For some of my plants I use copper saucepans which were originally found in a very old bakery; they were quite black when I bought them. My houseboy, Rengan, in Ceylon, used to clean our brass and copper with a mixture of salt and lemon so I decided to do the same with my saucepans – and with great success! They are now shining. I used the juice of one large lemon and a dessertspoon of sea salt mixed well. It is important to wear rubber gloves to protect your hands.

Tea pot

The above line drawing shows an attractive old English teapot which only needs a few trails of honeysuckle, jasmine or ivy flowing from it with perhaps two or three garden roses and few sweet peas. The lid can be taken off and placed beside the finished arrangement.

The Turkish coffee pot needs even fewer flowers – just some specimens of 'Golden Shower' orchids or a single stem of lilies.

Coffee pot

The copper kettle, also Turkish, would be attractive for a plant holder or a massed summer garden flower arrangement. One could use long marguerites and cow parsley, massed roses and sweet peas, or quite simply a round arrangement of marigolds and golden privet with ivy trails.

Kettle

Mug

The mug is ideal for a dressing table or at the bedside, and again takes just a few flowers, a handful of forget-me-nots or lily of the valley.

Containers

I use the shallow dish for an occasional Ikebana type design – a pinholder, a few flowers and a branch or two. It is also attractive as a plant container and I protect the copper by lining the dish with kitchen foil.

Dish

Curd pot.

One of my favourite copper containers is the Turkish curd pot which I used so much in California with trails of jasmine and clematis.

I keep all these containers bright by cleaning once every three months with the long term copper cleaning fluid and a soft duster.

General care and treatment of flowers

Spring and summer are the most exciting times for flower lovers. It is so important to cut carefully from the garden and countryside with thought, so that there is no waste of beautiful material. Great care should be taken when gathering wild flowers not to uproot any plant thus doing irreparable damage.

I usually sketch my arrangements and/or bouquets when planning the overall scheme. By doing this one has a definite plan and a grand total of requirements can easily be reached. This helps to speed up things when setting off to cut from the garden or buy from the florist.

On returning home cut all the flower stems at an angle (this gives a bigger drinking space and keeps the stem from being sealed off at the bottom of the container) and put into buckets of deep water. Hard stemmed flowers and woody foliage should be hammered or slit before going into water.

Ferns and large fleshy leaves like being submerged in a bath of water for one to two hours. Then cut and stand upright in water. A great many shrubs and woody stemmed flowers revive and last longer if given their first drink standing in warm water. Hammer or slit the stem ends and place in warm water. Mimosa, lilac, vibernum, hellebores and foxgloves are all in this category; all leaves of lilac and some larger viberum leaves should be removed as these tend to wilt quickly. Mimosa is now sold with packets of crystals which should be dissolved in their water to keep the blossom fluffy for several days even in central heating.

Many summer flowers appreciate sugar in their water. I usually mix two teaspoonsful of white sugar with $1\frac{3}{4}$ pints or 1 litre water. There is also a *Biolife* mixture on the market which has instructions for use with different varieties of flowers. As a general rule I find that it is the long spiky summer flowers, (lupins, larkspur, delphiniums, jasmin, sweet peas) which really do well and last longer in sugar. Roses also appreciate this drink as do wild flowers such as blue bells and cow parsley.

General care and treatment of flowers

Delphiniums and other hollow stemmed flowers should be turned upside down and filled with the mixture, then the stem ends plugged with cotton wool. In Ceylon I grew and used a great many amaryllis lilies. First I filled their large hollow stems with a support stick or stem of a slim palm, then the lily stem was filled with sugar water and finally plugged with cotton wool – they would last for days and days in this way.

In the tropics and California I used a great deal of bougainvillae. First the leaves are all stripped off and then the long sprays of colourful flowers are submerged in a bath of warm water. After two hours take out, hammer stems gently and place in buckets of deep water out of a draught.

Two other glorious vines which I also use and submerge in the same way are the blue *Petrea* 'Queen's Wreath' and mauve-pink *Congea* – both are so delicate and starlike, therefore ideal for pedestal arrangements which need flowers to cascade downwards.

Oleanders, euphorbia, poinsettia, frangipani, poppies and dahlias last longer if their stem ends are either held for a second over a flame or else dipped into boiling water for a minute. Another beautiful cascading flower which I like to use in large tropical arrangments is the *Datura* or 'Angel's Trumpet Tree'. All but the smallest leaves should be removed, the stem slit and a long deep drink given before arranging. *Datura*, like oleander, is POISONOUS so care must be taken if children are around. The perfume of the *Datura* is really exotic; it could be overbearing in a closed room but ideal for tropical homes where there are verandahs and wide open windows.

Longest lasting of all the tropical flowers are of course the various gingers, all of which I like to use whenever possible – the ostrich plume ginger, torch ginger and shell ginger, also the *Heliconia* 'Lobster Claw'. All these flowers grow almost hidden by their huge, heavy leaves so the leaves must be cut away and substituted by other more attractive ones. Stems should be slit and placed in very deep water for a long drink before arranging. *Spathiphyllium* is good to use but in the tropics, likes to be submerged for one to two hours with its own leaves for the initial treatment as it is delicate. It is similar in shape to the *Anthurium* but far more delicate looking.

In Bermuda, from my brother's garden, I used with great success the blooms of *Poinciana* 'Flame Tree', also the blooms of the orchid tree and hibiscus flowers. In all three cases I cut very early in the morning when the bloom was only half open, removed a great deal of leaf, soaked the stem for two hours in deep water then arranged in low bowls with sugar water. The *Poinciana* flowers lasted three or four days and the *Hibiscus* two days, and there was no problem adding fresh *Hibiscus* every two days as they were so plentiful. The pinky orchid like flowers of the orchid tree lasted for a week and gave great pleasure. A cube or two of ice can be added daily to the water in each container. This seems to refresh the flowers in hot weather, as of course, does a light spray each day.

Index